The Definitive Guide To Apartment Marketing

How To Generate More Leads, Close More
Leases & Improve Resident Experience

Josh Grillo

Want the Latest in Apartment Marketing?

There's a great deal of information covered in this book and many of these topics are discussed in depth in my weekly e-newsletter.

Join the community of over 4,000 multifamily professionals and get tips, tactics, and tutorials delivered to your inbox every Wednesday.

Visit **http://resident360.com/community** to check it out.

I'll see you there.

CONTENTS

INTRODUCTION

What's changed since I first sat down to write *The Definitive Guide To Apartment Marketing* and is it sufficient enough to warrant an update of this book?

If you've been involved in apartment marketing over the last few years then you can attest, that a ton of changes have occurred, and yet, much has remained the same.

The updates in this version of *The Definitive Guide To Apartment Marketing,* reflect many of these changes with regard to new strategies, tools, and tactics.

This updated version will help you build a better mousetrap for capturing leads, converting leases, and improving the resident experience.

We are in a highly technological age where your digital footprint is vital to your success in apartment marketing. You need a total web presence to survive and thrive.

You can no longer build, buy, or manage an apartment community, put out a "Now Leasing" sign, and expect the crowds to come running.

Just not happening. The lazy days of marketing apartments are over. Outdated websites, no online presence, sloppy leasing calls, lackluster community tours, poor resident service, lack of follow-up, bad execution—I could go on and on—those days are over.

If you want quality residents, you have to stand out and be, look, and act better than your competitors. You also need to be frequenting online locations and social media sites on the Internet where your potential residents are hanging out.

These days the prospective resident is king. All the power has returned to them and they know it. They can do a quick Google search for a new apartment. They are able to click on a few websites, look at photos, read reviews, and make assumptions, positive or negative. They can talk to a few friends and then decide if they want to pick up the phone and call you to schedule a tour.

If you do get that call, your salesmanship and follow-up skills have to be at an all-time high or you may leave the door open for a competitive community down the street to swoop in and get the lease.

That's why good marketing is so vital to the health of your community. It can bring you a steady stream of qualified prospects and can also help turn your existing residents into your best sales force.

In short, regardless of your experience in apartment marketing, my goal with this book is to give you a solid foundation of the terminology, strategies, and ideas for improving leads, leases, occupancy, and rent.

So… let's get started.

CHAPTER 1

WHAT IS YOUR MARKETING STRATEGY

What are you currently doing to market your community - posting Craigslist ads, relying on ILS, or Internet Listing Services like apartments.com, or spending money on SEO?

The problem I find with communities marketing their own apartments is there is no real consistency in what they do and no tracking in place to tell them if what they're doing is actually working. The marketing hat or role is usually worn by a property manager or group of employees who are also wearing a lot of other hats.

Even if you're a Marketing Director reading this book, your time may be splintered fifty different ways between new lease ups, websites, new software, existing communities, branding initiatives, strategy, meetings, and conferences.

As a result, the actual community marketing takes the approach of "It'll get done when it gets done." That's the unfortunate side of apartment marketing. It suffers from a lack of resources or, in some cases, too many resources with nobody managing the implementation.

It's important that every person involved in the marketing of your community actually understands and knows what you're trying to achieve. This is especially the case when you implement new software and tools to help automate the marketing process.

I've seen squandered hours and wasted dollars on great tools purchased by multifamily companies where nobody took the time to learn or, more importantly, manage.

At the end of the day, it comes down to resources:

- Who's doing the actual marketing?

- Do they understand your goals?

- Do they understand the tools, software, and strategy they've been given?

- Who's reviewing the data from this marketing to make informed decisions?

- And, who's overseeing it all?

These are all questions you need to ask yourself. As you move forward in the book, the answers will be revealed.

Let's start now by digging into your own marketing strategy. Here's what we want to take a look at:

1. Who is your ideal resident?

2. What makes your community different from those offered by your competitors?

3. What marketing/advertising should you be using to deliver your message?

4. What type of marketing budget should you set up?

5. What goals do you want to hit?

6. What collateral do you have?

7. How will you track what is and isn't working?

Let's break these down one at a time.

1. Who is your ideal resident?

Probably the biggest rule in successful marketing is you need to know exactly who you are marketing to if you're going to have a big impact. For example, a forty-year-old professional with a wife and two kids isn't going to be frequenting in the same places as a twenty-something.

The best way to identify your target market is by looking at the current residents you already have. Can you group them into certain personas? For example, you have a large group of working professionals. This group tends to like to work out, as you see them in the gym often. They're attractive, in shape, and they like to go out on the weekends. Most are in their thirties. What else do you know about them? They probably spend a lot of time online or on their cell phones. They may have a certain political affiliation. The goal here is to add in as many characteristics and traits (demographics) about this group as you can.

What you're creating is your ideal resident avatar.

A resident avatar is an individual with a name, a picture, and specific characteristics and traits. It's not a real specific person. It's just a composite of characteristics of many real people.

You are describing your target market, the prospects that you want most as your residents.

See how many other groups or avatars you can create based on your research. It's best to stick with your top two to three groups that represent the largest number of residents for marketing purposes.

Now that you know who your ideal resident is, you'll want to make sure your marketing reflects these people. In other words, you don't want to have a website with all senior citizens on it if you're marketing to young professionals.

Just be aware of Fair Housing Laws when it comes to photos and text in your marketing.

2. What makes your community different from those offered by your competitors?

I'm sure you've heard Domino's unique selling proposition (USP), "Fresh, hot pizza delivered in thirty minutes or less, or it's free." Domino's built their entire business on that USP and also by positioning themselves next to college campuses.

What makes you different? What makes your community unique?

If I was looking to rent an apartment in your area and visited five communities, including yours, what would make me say, "I'm choosing you." Please don't say you're the cheapest on the block. If you want to compete on price, that's fine, but here's a warning: *There will always be someone cheaper.*

This is where you can really have a big advantage over competitors. Yes, some people shop based on price and they want the cheapest place they can find to live in, but these may not be the type of residents you're looking for.

The advantage you gain lies in distinguishing some really cool, outside-the-box way in which you're unique.

Maybe you're like the national firm, BSB Design, and have pet pods built into your apartments. These are mini washrooms for pets, complete with a tiled floor, drain, and space for a dog crate. Maybe you're the highest-rated community in your area on apartmentratings.com or Yelp—that's a huge selling point. You offer package lockers or community-wide, free Wi-Fi, another great plus.

Just stop, take some time, and think about what makes your community unique and different. Once you have a list of items, make sure they're added to all your marketing materials and that your leasing agents know them, as well.

3. What marketing/advertising should you be using to deliver your message?

By now, you should know who your ideal resident is—basically who you're targeting with your marketing. You also know what makes you different and stand out.

Let's discuss how you're going to deliver your message to make the greatest impact and generate quality leads.

As you're probably aware, there are many types of marketing and advertising options available to you for delivering your message. Some are a waste of time while others work really well.

I recommend having a mix of both online and offline marketing/advertising as part of your overall strategy.

We'll go into this in much more detail in later chapters.

"MARKETING HAS MADE THE PACKAGING LARGER, REMOVED HALF THE CONTENTS, DOUBLED THE PRICE AND CALLED IT 'VERSION 2.0.' HAVE WE MISSED ANYTHING?"

4. What type of marketing budget should you set up?

Here are some stats from a survey done by Multifamily Insiders and Satisfacts on apartment marketing:

Average Marketing Budget
2016 = $41 per unit monthly
2015 = $23 per unit monthly

Average Cost Per Lead
2016 = $37
2015 = $52

Average Cost Per Lease
2016 = $296
2015 = $311

These numbers should give you an idea of what others are doing. When you look at where you should invest your money, the first place to start is your community website. This will be the hub of all your marketing and information—probably the first place a prospective resident will visit—so it pays to have a quality, easy-to-navigate, and fast-loading website in place.

5. What goals do you want to hit?

If you don't know where you're going, how are you going to get there?

The truth about marketing is you need to have attainable, reachable, and measurable goals. Obviously, you want more quality leads, leases, better occupancy, and higher rents, but can you put a number and more importantly a date to it? For example, aiming for and maintaining ninety-six percent occupancy is a great goal. Getting your cost per lead and lease down is another good one.

6. What collateral do you have?

Take a few minutes and inventory your collateral. Make sure your logo, brochure, and, more importantly, community photos are the best possible.

When reviewing your community photos, ask yourself the following:

- Do I have enough good quality shots? (I don't think you can overdo it with the number of photos you show. More is better in this case, if they are quality.)

- Do I have several photos of the main selling features of our community (Example: Fitness Center, Resort Style Pool, Modern Kitchens)

- Are inside apartment shots staged?

- Do outside shots highlight the best areas of the community?

- Do I show local neighborhood shots?

If you need new photos, hire a photographer who specializes in real estate photography. They will know how to get the best shots that feature your community to its fullest potential and in the best light.

Photographer pricing differs by city and availability; however, bigger cities will more than likely have good photographers at competitive prices. Here's a money saving tip: If you're in a college town, you might be able to get a free student photographer to help build their portfolio.

If you have a photographer coming out to your community, here's a quick checklist to make sure you have everything covered:

- ✓ Community Manager alerted
- ✓ List of areas to shoot
- ✓ Community outside areas swept and cleaned
- ✓ Staged apartment with raked rug
- ✓ Good lighting conditions
- ✓ Pool area concrete hosed for wet, glossy look

> **PRO TIP**: Make sure they shoot photographs of the neighborhood, especially local hot spots.

In addition to having great pictures, you need a high-quality brochure that showcases these images, text about why you're different, rates, floor plan examples, contact information, and any other additional items you deem important.

To accompany your photos and brochure, you want to make sure you have a website that reflects your marketing.

Your community website should be the hub of all your information. I can't state how important this is. Everything should start and stop at your website. It is the most valuable marketing tool you have available and it pays to do it right.

I talk about the community website throughout this book and devote Chapter 5 to it, so make sure you read that chapter.

The last thing I want to mention here is organization. I've worked with many properties that have their information scattered all over the place. Where are the photos? What are the passwords to the accounts? Where can I find the email addresses for leads? The list goes on and on.

Does this sound familiar?

It's best you begin organizing your marketing material now. Start by putting everything in one place: photos, passwords, email addresses, contacts, documents, you name it.

This could be a file folder, an online notebook like Evernote, Google Docs, Dropbox (I use it and love it), or some other secure online space. Just organize it so you have it all in one place. It will make your life and business practices easier and more successful.

7. How will you track what is and isn't working?

Companies are trying to get better at tracking leads and leases to track return on investment (ROI) and conversion rates. There are software solutions out there to help, but there is no magic bullet. It's fairly easy to implement lead tracking where you can put a dynamic call tracking number and unique email on every advertising source. This will allow you to pull data and see what advertising sources are producing leads.

For example, your website would have a unique call tracking phone number and unique email address. Your Craigslist ads would have a unique call tracking phone number and unique email address. Any direct mail like postcards would have a unique call tracking phone number and unique email address.

The true beauty of this is at any given time you can run a report to see how a particular marketing source or campaign is working for you. How many leads did your website generate today? How many inquiries were phone calls versus emails?

To take it a step further, you can implement a lead management solution. Lead management tracks the lead from inception all the way to the point of signing a lease.

Think of it as handholding for a lead. The lead comes in and the leasing agent knows exactly the source and medium where it was generated and what should be the follow-up process.

The beauty of lead management is you can usually run robust reports giving you details on conversions, letting you know who your top leasing agents are, and what are the top lead-to-lease sources. This is all incredible data that lets you know what's working and what's not. The key is you need to review this data on a consistent basis to make it effective for you, your business, and your sales team.

In the next chapter, we'll dive into generating high-quality leads for your community.

Want the Latest in Apartment Marketing?

There's a great deal of information covered in this book and many of these topics are discussed in depth in my weekly e-newsletter.

Join the community of over 4,000 multifamily professionals and get tips, tactics, and tutorials delivered to your inbox every Wednesday.

Visit **http://resident360.com/community** to check it out.

I'll see you there.

CHAPTER 2

HOW TO GENERATE QUALITY LEADS

There are hundreds of ways to generate leads, but when you think about high-quality ones that turn into leases, it comes down to doing a few things really well.

Let's start by taking a look at the data on how today's residents are searching for apartments:

> Fifty-four percent (54%) of residents consulted an opinion website on which communities to visit and where to rent.

> Seventy-three percent (73%) of residents searched at least one Internet Listing Service (ILS) when hunting for an apartment.

> Fifty-two percent (52%) decided not to visit a community after reading a poor online review.

> ➤ Eighty percent (80%) of residents searched for an apartment by visiting community websites.

Source: 2015 Renter Preferences Study by Kingsley Associates and NMHC

At my company, Resident360, we work with hundreds of communities on generating leads. Strategies and what works best change over time as new products and tools are introduced into the marketplace. I've put together a list below of areas you should pay attention to:

- Community Website

- Live Chat

- Craigslist

- Google Adwords (Includes Search, Geo-Targeting, and Remarketing)

- Google My Business (formerly Google Places)

- Drive By

- Email Marketing

- Internet Listing Services

- Resident Referrals

- Direct Mail – Postcards

- Community Videos

- Live Streaming

- Search Engine Optimization (SEO)

- Content Marketing

- Social Media

- Resident Events

To help you to better understand what may work best for your communities, let's break each one down, covering some of the positives and strategies for success.

COMMUNITY WEBSITE

As I've said before, a community website is the best source for high-quality leads that turn into leases, provided of course, you have a great website.

If you had to choose only one thing to put money into, I would strongly recommend starting with your community website. This should be the hub of all your marketing. Plus, it's the first impression visitors may get of your community.

Spend the money and get yourself something nice that represents your demographic and also what you're trying to achieve internally. A great community website will make your community more valuable. I do a full write-up in Chapter 5 on community websites, so make sure you spend some time reading that chapter.

LIVE CHAT

I'm a big fan of having Live Chat on your community website. Live Chat is not rocket science, but there are a few key things you need to know if you ever intend to implement it on your own website.

Here Are Three Keys To Making Live Chat Work For You:

Key #1 - You Need To Manage It

Someone on your staff will have to become a Live Chat operator and be prepared to engage visitors who are on your website. It's actually quite fun and you'd be surprised at how many people will chat with you.

PRO TIP: I occasionally man the Live Chat on Resident360.com because I want to get real-time insight as to what my website visitors are saying over chat. This is valuable data.

Key #2 - Fifteen Second Pop-Up

Get a Live Chat program that will ping the visitor after so many seconds of being on your website. For example: I'm visiting your website and after fifteen seconds of being on the site, the Live Chat window pops up and the operator asks how they can help me. This keeps your site interactive and chances are high website visitors will engage with your Live Chat operator.

Key #3 - Target Your Message

Have targeted questions/responses for whatever page the prospect is on. For example, if someone is on the Floor

Plans page, you could have your Live Chat operator ask, "Are you interested in a one, two, or three bedroom today?" Using a targeted message like this will give you a higher probability of engaging the prospect versus simply saying, "Hi, how can I help you?"

As awesome as Live Chat is as a marketing tool, the reality is someone has to manage it full time. Otherwise, you're wasting money. A fully managed solution will give you operators working on your behalf, selling the benefits of your community twenty-four hours a day, seven days a week. Your website will become more interactive and you'll gain an upper hand in generating leads.

One issue that comes up with fully managed solutions is quality control. You need to make sure the operators are saying the right things about your community. This can be controlled easily by supplying the right information about your community upfront and testing the Live Chat as you're a prospective resident searching for a new apartment.

CRAIGSLIST

There are many strategies for posting apartments on Craigslist and I think your best tactic is to use more than one angle. It's not rocket science to grasp that varied demographics will be drawn to different content in a title. Although we all want to rent to employed, responsible people that still results in a wide range of demographics.

In order to engage with as wide a range as possible, try posting for the same vacant unit with three entirely different titles. (Although I'm focusing on the title, remember, in order to avoid "ghosting," the content of the post cannot be exactly the same in all three.) If you're unfamiliar with the term ghosting here's a quick definition: Ghosting is when your ads appear to have posted successfully, but Craigslist actually hides these ads from users. Craigslist is tricking you into believing your ads are posted when in reality, they are not.

One way to approach this is to give each title a specific focus. For example:

1. One title could focus on the interior of the specific unit.

2. One or two titles could focus on the location and/or community amenities.

3. Another title could be almost random, intended to draw in anyone on Craigslist who is tired of searching and looking at boring titles.

4. If you are offering any concessions, that can be an additional title or combined with one of the tactics above.

More specifically, the above suggestions might look like this:

West Facing Balcony, Lots of Natural Light, Garage, D/W, A/C – PETS WELCOME

This will appeal to the person who is scanning Craigslist almost exclusively interested in the interior details of a specific apartment home. They are less interested in the pool and fitness center because they are at first attracted to information about the actual apartment they may live in.

2BR/2BA in Smith School District – Affordable & Available Now

Mentioning the school district is an entirely underutilized angle. Do not miss out on the segment of apartment searchers who are looking to move into a particular district. They can be great, long-term residents.

1 BR Easy Tollway Access AND Near the Smith Golf Course

This is an example of location focus. Obviously, location is an easy one, but remember not to focus exclusively on location. For many renters, price and interiors are more important and you don't want to miss out on attracting those people too.

1 BR Easy Access to Downtown, Sign a Lease Today & Get 2 Weeks Free

This appeals to the busy person who commutes, just wants to get the apartment search over with, and wouldn't mind saving a few bucks.

Love the local farmer's market? We do too.

This is the type of title that might simply make a prospective resident curious. It will catch their eye and stand out. The unit you're advertising may not be right for them, but they may go to your website and see you also have exactly what they were looking for.

Gangnam Style in Downtown

This is almost in the silly category. In case you're unaware, this title refers to a popular hip-hop song that went viral on social media. Using a well-placed lyric or pop culture reference can be extremely effective if your apartment community targets college students or tends to draw the single professional crowd.

It's important to remember that what would make you want to click on a link and read the post is not the same thing that would draw in someone else. When you mix up the features, you are promoting, it can really increase your leads and give you more prospective residents interested in your community.

Use Keywords in the Body of Your Ads

One great way to make sure your Craigslist ads get seen more is to use a keyword paragraph at the bottom of your ads. This will help you show up when apartment hunters do a specialized search on Craigslist. For example, I search, "3 bedroom apartment by the beach." If you have the keywords 3 bedroom, apartment, and beach anywhere in your ad, you're more than likely going to show up.

The idea here is to think of every keyword that could be attributed to your community.

Focus on location, floor plan types, amenities, pets, cross streets, and even landmarks. For example, here's a keyword group you could use in your ads (obviously, you want to replace the words that don't make sense for your community).

Pacific Palms Apartments, apartments for rent, dog, cat, CA, gated community, pet friendly, Ocean Beach, bike room, laundry facility, apartments in san diego, 1 bedroom, 2 bedroom, studio, 1br, 2br, playground, pets, seaworld, san diego zoo, i-8 freeway, military, discount

PRO TIP: You can also add your competitor's names to this list if you want to show up when someone searches for them on Craigslist.

GOOGLE ADWORDS

Google Adwords is a fantastic advertising service for communities wanting to display ads on Google and its advertising network. With Adwords, you can set a budget for your advertising and only pay when people click on your ads.

At Resident360, we've had great success driving leads for communities through the following campaign types in Adwords:

- Search campaigns
- Geo-Targeting campaigns
- Remarketing campaigns

Let's break down each one in depth.

Search Campaigns

You know when you do a Google search and you see ads at the very top and bottom of the page? That's a search campaign setup through Adwords.

How does it work? Put briefly, you use their platform to create ads, and then bid on search terms or keywords where you want these ads to show up.

It's a fast and relatively inexpensive way to get your website at the top of Google search results whenever someone searches for an apartment in your area.

You're charged when someone clicks on your ad (CPC or Cost Per Click). The cost varies on how competitive the keyword is and how well your search campaign is optimized. On average, it could be as low as fifty cents a click to well over $5 a click.

An effective Adwords strategy is to set an annual budget for your community. Let's say you want to spend $3,600 over the entire year. That will give you a $300 a month budget for clicks. Instead of dedicating the entire $300 every month (like many communities do), fluctuate the budget over the year. In slower months, like late fall and winter, up the budget to $500 - $600 a month to give you more traffic. Then, slowly take it back down to $100 - $200 in good months, like spring, summer, and early fall. You'll still be spending your $3,600 annual budget, but you'll be doing it in a way that keeps traffic consistent year-round at your community.

> **PRO TIP**: Write your ad copy centered on units you have available.

Geo-Targeting Campaigns

With a Geo-Targeting campaign in Adwords, you can target prospects in geographic areas near your community.

Imagine drawing a one-mile radius around your community and targeting all those people who are online with your ads.

Or imagine drawing a circle around large employers in your area and targeting those people with your ads.

That can be done with Geo-Targeting through Adwords and it's extremely inexpensive.

For example, at Resident360, we've run Geo-Targeting campaigns for communities with cost per click prices at around ten cents a click. The key to running these campaigns is to make sure you offer a strong incentive to come tour your community. This needs to be displayed on your ads.

It's definitely worth testing out for your own community.

Remarketing Campaigns

Remarketing brings prospects back to you. It's activated when the prospective resident leaves your website and visits other websites. They'll be served up your advertisements on some of those websites as if they're being surrounded by your community. This works well in getting the prospective resident back to your website and offers up valuable community branding keeping you top of mind. It's also very cost-effective.

> **PRO TIP**: Create a "Welcome Back" page on your community website for when a prospective resident clicks on your remarketing ad. Give them an additional incentive to tour your community. Write your ad copy centered on units you have available.

Wrapping Up Adwords

To show you how effective Google Adwords can be, let me share with you one month's data from one of our communities. Pay attention to how low the cost per click price is for each campaign.

- 30 Day Adwords Campaign
- Search Campaign CPC = $0.86
- Remarketing Campaign CPC = $0.17
- Geo-Targeting Campaign CPC = $0.06
- 2,262 Total Campaign Clicks
- $588.22 Monthly Cost

GOOGLE MY BUSINESS
(FORMERLY GOOGLE PLACES)

Google My Business helps you get your community hours, phone number, and directions on Google Search and Maps.

It's also incredibly important for local SEO. Local SEO helps you rank higher on map listings when someone does a Google search. Here are some tips for optimizing your Google My Business listing to give you the most exposure:

- First, claim your listing, by going to http://google.com/business

- Ensure your details are up-to-date

- Double-check your opening hours and phone number(s)

- Pick a picture that will make your listing stand out and get clicked

- Check the images you are using and consider refreshing them

- Choose the "Apartment Building" category

- Get residents to post reviews

- Get citations or listings in directories like Yelp, Citysearch, InfoUSA, and even ILS websites like apartments.com, forrent.com, and apartmentguide.com.

- Make sure your community name, address, and phone number, called NAP, are the same on these directory style sites

DRIVE BY

Since you have a physical location, it's in your best interest to do everything in your power to make sure the community stands out to people driving by.

So how do you make your community stand out? The first thing you should do is have massive signs with something as simple as "Now Leasing" on them.

If you are right next to a busy road, consider having a series of signs that highlight a benefit like "Spacious Floor Plans" or "Move-In Special Happening Now." The key is to make the sign huge, with bold lettering and not much text, so it's easy to spot and more importantly read when someone is driving by.

Additionally, I'm a fan of balloons. A lot of them. Why? Because balloons are nostalgic, they signal a party, a celebration, and most people want to go to a party.

Balloons also raise curiosity. Have you ever driven down the street where you live and seen balloons on a mailbox or fence, and then wondered what they have going on? I bet you have. Balloons do that.

The last thing on the drive by is to make sure your community is always in tip-top shape. I know I don't have to tell you this, but some people may need a reminder.

Grounds should be manicured and swept. It should always look like a well-kept community with fantastic curb appeal. Couple that with multiple big signs, balloons, and one of those sign twirler guys and you'll see action.

EMAIL MARKETING

It's important to be collecting the email address of every prospect who reaches out to you. It's also important to collect the email addresses of your existing residents.

These email addresses should be added to some type of customer management software or email management system for marketing purposes.

There are several good ones out there like Constant Contact, Mailchimp, Aweber, Infusionsoft, Hubspot, and Salesforce. Additionally, some of the property management software packages offer email marketing capabilities.

With the right email management system in place, you can do the following:

You can create an automated follow-up sequence (series of emails) for prospects that includes special offers, discounts, and multiple calls to actions to entice the prospective resident to get back in touch with you.

You can send personal follow-up emails to prospects, answering their questions and see if they actually open that email.

You can send an email blast to all residents letting them know about a future community event.

At Resident360, we've had good success by sending out a monthly email blast to prospects updating them on the construction of a new development. We call these prospects our VIPs.

STRATEGY FOR EFFECTIVE EMAIL MARKETING

How can you make your emails more interesting to prospects?

Start by looking at the first email you send to them and ask yourself the question—is this email personal or does it come across as generic?

This is important.

You want that first email to be personal. Make it a quick note to say "hello," and, more importantly, introduce yourself. This will raise your chances of catching the prospect's attention and they are more likely to respond.

For example, at Resident360, our goal is to be more personal in our emails. What we're working on is shooting a quick iPhone video where I would introduce myself to a prospective client who reached out through email.

Take that video, embed it in an email, and then send it to the prospective client. This takes a bit of technical know-how, but it's definitely doable for a tech-minded person.

Here are a few other tips:

Use the prospect's first name only when reaching out - You don't need the first and last name together or Mr. and Mrs. This makes it more personal.

Keep it short - Be respectful of other people's time. Short, to the point emails get read.

Ask open-ended questions in your email - Are you more interested in an end unit or a unit with a pool view?

Timing is everything – You must be quick when you receive an email from a prospective resident. They're checking out everyone else as well. Be the first to respond and be personal.

INTERNET LISTING SERVICES

An Internet Listing Service (ILS) is basically an online directory that features apartments. The best examples are apartments.com and apartmentguide.com.

Typically, you pay a monthly premium to have your community listed on an ILS. The benefit is that the ILS already has built-in traffic with many prospective residents searching the site for apartments.

So basically, you're paying to list your community on the website in hopes of getting some of those people to check out your community.

Some ILSs have a pay per lease model while others just charge a flat monthly fee. You will need to do some research to find which one works best for you in your area.

When you decide to put your community on an ILS there are a few things you need to take into consideration. First, you're lumped together with all your competitors. Knowing this going into it, you have to make sure your listing stands out.

IF YOU WANT TO CATCH A LOT
OF FISH... YOU HAVE TO USE THE
RIGHT BAIT

How do you do that?

The photos you choose to display are extremely important. The majority of shots you want to showcase should be your best outdoor photos coupled with a few indoor shots. Your cover shot or the photo that goes on the front of your listing should be your best outside pool photo. If you don't have a pool, pick something that just looks beautiful.

Remember, photos rent apartments. So, put your absolute best photo up front.

A compelling description for your community is your next priority. If you look around, most properties just have a blob of hard to read text. I've found that answering the three questions below gives a better description than most of your competitors. Obviously, you'll want to elaborate a little more than my example answers:

- What do I have?

    - Modern spacious apartments within walking distance of great restaurants and shopping

- How will it benefit a prospective resident?

    - More room for you to unwind, relax, and be comfortable

    - Have fun with your friends as you can walk to great restaurants and entertainment

- What do I want the prospective resident to do next?

  - Schedule a tour today by calling or filling out the contact form on this page

Finally, once you have your ILS listing set up, it's important you review it for accuracy. That means testing phone numbers and making sure they ring to your community. Don't skip this step. I can't tell you how many times I've reviewed ILS listings only to find out they had the wrong phone number for the community.

RESIDENT REFERRALS

A resident referral is the best type of lead you can get because most turn into leases. If an existing resident is recommending their apartment community to a friend, family member, or colleague, chances are the person is already sold on your community.

All you need to do is make sure you manage that lead properly with the highest regard and best follow-up. That means greeting this referral with a warm smile and a beverage. Take them on a well-rehearsed tour of your community and mail them a handwritten thank-you letter.

If you implement these steps for every person who tours your properties, not just referrals, you'll see an improvement in lease conversion.

Additionally, resident referrals really go hand in hand with resident renewals. A resident isn't going to refer your community if they're not happy with where they live. That goes for renewing their lease, as well.

DIRECT MAIL - POSTCARDS

Direct mail, such as postcards, can be very effective when done right. Unfortunately, many try it once and give up because they don't see the results.

I've seen several communities have success using oversized postcards. This is an affordable option for mailing in select zip codes by your community.

Here are a few more tips:

- ✓ Make sure to use an easy to read font like Arial, Times New Roman, or even consider handwritten fonts as these stand out.

- ✓ Have captivating photos with a headline below each photo.

- ✓ Have a clear call to action with an offer and deadline.

- ✓ Have a clear way to respond with the community phone number and website in big, bold font.

COMMUNITY VIDEOS

I think it's safe to say that both of us know the popularity of video. YouTube is the second largest search engine in the world behind Google. That alone is monumental in terms of the consumption of video.

With so many different video styles being offered today, what's best for your community?

Let's examine the Pros and Cons of each...

#1 Virtual Tour Style

Virtual tours are almost in a category of their own, as they're not quite a video. The virtual tour is navigated by the end user clicking a mouse around on a floor plan or swiping a finger on a mobile phone.

Pros: Cost-effective, interactive, and unique. Makes sense if you want to have individual floor plan tours. Fairly inexpensive, averaging $550 a tour.

Cons: Usually don't show the community as a whole. Restricted to floor plans.

#2 Spokesperson Style

Spokesperson style videos are becoming more popular in multifamily as they give you an actual narrated, first person walking tour of a community.

Pros: Easy to showcase the big benefits of the community. Not limited to just a floor plan. You can share on other video sites like YouTube and Vimeo.

Cons: They can be expensive, averaging $4,000-$5,000 a video. Your prospects might not relate to the spokesperson in your video.

#3 Drone Style

Drone style videos are awesome if you have a large community with a resort style feel. A drone flies over the community, shooting Hi-Def footage, combined with on the ground footage to make a visually pleasing apartment video.

Pros: Gives the prospect a 360-degree look at your community. Unique and visually stunning.

Cons: Somewhat expensive, averaging $3,000 a video.

#4 Lifestyle

If you have a luxury community commanding high rents, then it's worth investing in a lifestyle video. A lifestyle video utilizes models and actors for showcasing different amenities your community offers. This usually includes the local neighborhood as well.

Pros: Probably the highest quality video you can get for your community. If you want to showcase "The Lifestyle," this is for you.

Cons: Roughly costing around $15,000.

#5 Slideshow Style

We've all seen examples of slideshow style videos. This is basically a slideshow of your photos mixed with text and music.

Pros: Inexpensive, usually under $500. A quick way to showcase good photos.

Cons: Can come across as outdated and cheap, if not done properly. Bad photos will make a bad video.

Three things to consider when looking at which video style is right for you:

1. What type of community do you have?

A luxury community can stand out with a drone style video. A C-grade community doesn't really need video.

2. What's the quality of your marketing?

If you're not investing in marketing at all, then don't start with a video.

3. What's your budget?

This will dictate for the most part which direction you go.

LIVE STREAMING

What if you could easily take the prospect on a community tour by launching an app on your phone and letting them see the product live through a video stream?

This is happening now in multifamily.

Two apps make this possible—Periscope and Meerkat. I'm a bigger fan of Periscope because it allows your audience (viewers) to interact with your live broadcast. They can send live comments directly to the phone you're broadcasting from.

If it sounds a little technical, it's not. Here are the steps to make this happen:

1. Download Periscope app from app store (it's free).

2. Launch app and test doing a live broadcast.

3. Promote to your prospect list through email and social media that you'll be doing a live community tour at a designated time. Periscope is connected to a Twitter account, so when you do a live broadcast a link to it will appear in your Twitter feed.

4. Launch Periscope and do a live broadcast at the designated time.

5. Rinse and repeat.

Woods Residential executed this strategy on their Alta Brookhaven community. Here were the results:

- 10,698 Twitter impressions on day of event
- #AltaBrookhaven reached 92,401 people
- 74 Viewers joined the live broadcast

Source: Units Magazine November 2015 Edition "Going With The Stream."

Best Practices for Live Streaming

1. Practice your community tour in advance

2. Consider having a co-worker with you to point out certain amenities

3. Have a strong call to action in your live broadcast

4. Promote, promote, promote in advance

> **PRO TIP**: Facebook Live was introduced at the time of writing this book. This could be an additional live stream platform that may be even easier than the two apps mentioned above.

SEARCH ENGINE OPTIMIZATION (SEO)

Search engine optimization (SEO) is the act of getting your website to rank for certain keywords in search results. For example, getting your community website to rank on the first page of Google search results for the term, "Apartments for rent in Cincinnati." Prospective residents find your listing in the search results, click on your website, and then you have the opportunity of capturing them as a lead. I go more in depth on this in Chapter 6.

CONTENT MARKETING

Content marketing is the act of creating good valuable content in many forms and having it appear in different places on the web that potentially target your prospective resident. It's very powerful, but not easy.

The content directs links back to your website, which, in turn, can help improve your search engine rankings and help you acquire new residents. Content can be in the form of articles, videos, audio, slides, and infographics so it can reach audiences on all channels.

For example, at Resident360, we write high-quality 1,500 word articles that we post for our clients on their community websites. Then, we syndicate these articles on Facebook and Twitter. This is content marketing.

Since the majority of your prospective residents are coming from the local area, you want to keep your content focused locally. Articles highlighting trendy restaurants, coffee shops, places to shop, and parks in the area will work well at capturing local traffic.

> **PRO TIP**: Quality over Quantity - It's not about how many pieces of content you produce. It's about the quality of those pieces.

SOCIAL MEDIA

Social Media can contribute to lead generation and help your website rank better in the search engines with the proper plan in place.

Let's break down social media into two parts:

Part 1 - Social Media Organic

Social media really goes hand in hand with content marketing. Any time you create valuable noteworthy content, you want to share it with different social media channels like Facebook, Google+, Twitter, and even YouTube. This helps you build your digital footprint.

Plus, new social media platforms are always emerging, like Snapchat, Periscope, Instagram, and Pinterest. It can be a little difficult to keep up with, but don't forget the following:

If people think the content is valuable, it will spread among their friends and family and drive more traffic back to your website and your social media page. This gives you more exposure and an opportunity to convert more prospects into actual leads.

For example, I could post a cute dog photo on the community's Facebook page with text that references our doggy blog for residents. This would get a bunch of Facebook likes and comments, and appear in the Facebook

SOCIAL IRONY

feed of more than just the fans of the community's page. A friend of a friend sees the post, has a dog, and is looking for a new place to live. This may, in fact, get them excited enough to click over to the community's website. At that point, it's up to the website to convert the prospect into a lead. Now do you see how social media can work for you?

I believe a Facebook page is best used for cultivating your community and updating your residents. Knowing this, you have to have a posting strategy in place. How many times a week are you going to post? What are those posts going to be about? It's a good idea to plan it out a month in advance. You also have to remember if anything goes wrong at your community that affects residents, one of the first places they're going to go to vent their frustrations is your Facebook page.

Part 2 - Social Media Advertising (Buying ads)

Social media advertising is buying ads on the different platforms such as Facebook, Instagram, and Twitter. The beauty of buying ads is you can really pinpoint your exact audience and it's pretty inexpensive. The key is you just have to test different ads and platforms.

For example, at Resident360, we're running several Facebook advertising campaigns for communities. My thoughts on the platform are this—Facebook is excellent for keeping your community top of mind while delivering tons of inexpensive, qualified traffic.

Here are some sample stats from one community:

Campaign Length: Thirty (30) Days

- 19,852 Ad Impressions for Community
- 515 Clicks to Community Website
- $96 Total Cost (19 cents a click)

> **PRO TIP**: Using long-form copy (lots of text) in Facebook Ads delivered the best response. Make sure to test this vs. short-form copy.

RESIDENT EVENTS

Even more important than having a slick social media strategy is having a consistent plan to enable your residents to connect in person with their neighbors and on-site staff. You can't make people be friends. However, you can create environments that allow them the opportunity to build connections with other people in their apartment community.

As with most things that are win-win for everyone, it's bound to benefit your NOI, ROI, and bottom line. I bet there's a study somewhere that would confirm what you already know—if people feel connected to their neighbors, they are more likely to renew their lease and become the kind of long-term residents who don't drop trash on the stairwell. The kind of resident who takes ownership of where they live and contributes to sustaining an environment that benefits residents and the owner. When neighbors connect, it's good for business and simply just good for people.

Although Facebook and Twitter are worthwhile endeavors for apartment communities, I believe they should never be more important than planning and implementing activities that help residents connect with each other in real life. It's not just the millennial generation that experiences social media over-saturation. I remember my first experience in a chat room. That was circa 1994, I think. Remember the dial up sound? Well, the novelty is over. People are seriously craving meaningful face-to-face interactions with other humans. You can give them what they want and the benefit goes both ways.

Make sure you're not planning only the kinds of resident events that require someone to be an outgoing lover of small talk.

Not everyone will be inclined to join a potluck or a meet and greet. Obviously, it's not your job to be everyone's friend, treat a resident activity like an extreme networking event, or cater to every interest and preference. You can lead the horse to water, no need to force them to drink. However, make sure there's more than one avenue to offer them the water if they are thirsty.

Consider finding one resident interested in leading a Walking Club. They could meet every other Saturday with no need for a staff member to be involved. If you have a clubhouse with a television, host a monthly movie night or game night. Events that have an actual activity (instead of just standing around and chatting) can be less threatening for new people or certain personality types.

Is your community near a walking trail or public park? Organize a quarterly volunteer day and pick up trash. Find out if there's an "Adopt a Park" program in your area. It could be a great way to show (and actually have) a commitment to the local community. Once again, not only is this good PR for your multifamily image, but also a genuine benefit for the area.

For me, there's a whole other element that has nothing to do with business. I just like the idea of people being a little less lonely and having a few more meaningful friendships in their life, even if it didn't happen to have a side effect like boosting resident retention. Being able to influence the environment where people live in a positive way is just a good thing. Period.

Plan some great events. Use social media to spread the word, remind residents, and follow-up with pictures or other comments after the event. Don't put all your energy into cultivating an online community if your in-person community is where your efforts are really needed.

In summary, there are many different things you can do to generate high-quality leads for your community. I would consider putting your website as the first priority. This should be your best mousetrap for capturing prospective residents and turning them into leads.

Want the Latest in Apartment Marketing?

There's a great deal of information covered in this book and many of these topics are discussed in depth in my weekly e-newsletter.

Join the community of over 4,000 multifamily professionals and get tips, tactics, and tutorials delivered to your inbox every Wednesday.

Visit **http://resident360.com/community** to check it out.

I'll see you there.

CHAPTER 3

HOW TO CLOSE MORE LEASES

There are three things holding you back from closing more leases:

1. The telephone
2. Your follow-up
3. Your community tour

Let's start by talking about the phone.

Businesses blow it when it comes to fresh hot prospects calling in for the first time. The first call is to obtain information to help them make a decision on something.

In these instances, businesses in general, don't know how to answer the phone properly and coach, YES coach, a prospect into their business. Most of the people answering the phone are order takers.

The same thing goes for the apartment industry. You have leasing agents who are great and others who may need help.

What you want to do is listen to your leasing calls. In most cases, these calls can be recorded if you're using lead tracking or management software. Listening to these calls will reveal everything you need to know about your agents and your processes.

Remember, if you have a prospect on the phone, THEY ARE INTERESTED. It's now up to you to sell them on why you're the best place to call home.

Now, I'm not a phone coach, but what I do recommend is that all leasing agents subscribe to the train of thought of "Goal Oriented Selling."

This means they need to focus on one goal when talking with prospects—to get the prospect to schedule a tour. By having this goal of the tour constantly in the back of their minds, it will really help get more tours booked.

Another important recommendation I have is focusing on tonality. Tonality is basically the act of raising and lowering your voice in conversation.

Most people don't want to talk to a boring, unexcited person on the other end of the phone. Have your agents add some personality and some excitement to their tone of voice. Have them show interest in the prospect and interest in the apartment.

This will help engage callers more and in some cases even get them excited. Think about this—you are not the first community the prospect has called. They've probably already talked to a few boring people on the phone. A call to your community is exactly what they need to get them motivated. This is a very good thing.

> **PRO TIP**: Try leasing through Skype. If your prospects have questions, get them on a Skype video conversation to address them. You're building more rapport with the prospect in a unique way.

WHAT IS YOUR FOLLOW-UP PLAN?

A prospect has shown interest by emailing, calling, or stopping by your community. What type of follow-up process do you have in place to convert this prospect into a resident?

A good follow-up process consists of multiple forms of contact like email, phone calls, text messages, and even direct mail. It's important to be pleasantly persistent with your follow-up, so your community stays top of mind with the prospect.

For example, you can set up a series of auto response emails that are sent out every day for five days straight, highlighting a "UNIQUE" special just for the prospect.

Additionally, follow-up with a series of phone calls and mail a handwritten thank-you note. This may sound like a great amount of work, but keep in mind you are showing the prospect you want his or her business.

Don't make the mistake of doing nothing, and never rely on just one form of follow-up.

WHAT HAPPENS WHEN A PROSPECTIVE RESIDENT TOURS YOUR COMMUNITY?

This is even more important than listening to leasing calls, because you have a prospective resident coming in to check out the community. The lead doesn't get any hotter than this, so you have to pull out all the stops to make sure you get their application.

Your staff must bring their "A" game. That means they need to look sharp, put on a huge smile, and have a positive, uplifting, excited attitude. Greet the prospect with a nice firm handshake, offer them a beverage, and begin your sales presentation. As you're fully aware, first impressions are everything. Here are some questions you should be asking yourself:

- What is your process when a prospect comes for a tour of your community?
- How is the prospect greeted?
- Are they given anything, like a beverage?
- What type of tour do you take them on?

- Is it a well-rehearsed tour by your best leasing agent?

Your tour should be well thought out in advance, rehearsed so it sounds natural, and obviously should highlight the most important benefits of living in your community.

Think about how you can make your tour different from all your competitors so you stand out. Why not offer a nice beverage and possibly a lunch coupon for a restaurant down the street.

Earlier, I mentioned "Goal Oriented Selling." The same thing goes for your community tour. Agents must focus on the goal of getting the application.

Ask the Hard Question

I've found that this particular question (below), when asked in any type of sales environment, can arm you with valuable data for helping convert a lead to lease.

The Question:

On a scale of one to ten, how serious are you in choosing our community?

Wait for their answer... then follow-up with:

What would make it a ten?

The prospective resident will more than likely reveal what it may take to get the lease done. Now you're armed with valuable data that may give you an upper hand in closing more leads into leases.

THE SHOCK AND AWE TOUR

Here is another strategy to help you close more leases, and one you may not have heard or thought of. Let me explain.

Have you ever received something totally unexpected in the mail that made you think, "Wow, that's really awesome. I can't believe they sent me something like that." Then you go tell your family, friends, and colleagues about it.

This is shock and awe marketing. Giving somebody something that makes them talk about you.

Why not create shock and awe for your community tour? Take a prospect on a tour of your community and end with a shock and awe package.

This package can contain:

- Starbucks gift card
- Handwritten thank-you note
- Scratch-off lottery ticket
- Candle, tape measure, candy
- Discounts to local stores
- Local area guide

You are now leaving a lasting impression in the prospect's mind and this goes a long way in getting the lease.

PRO TIP: Spotlight your leasing agents on your community website. This way, prospective residents can start a relationship with you before they come to the property. When they do show up, they'll already be familiar with the leasing agent. Spotlighting your leasing agents can be as simple as having a page that has their headshot and a short Q & A about them.

Want the Latest in Apartment Marketing?

There's a great deal of information covered in this book and many of these topics are discussed in depth in my weekly e-newsletter.

Join the community of over 4,000 multifamily professionals and get tips, tactics, and tutorials delivered to your inbox every Wednesday.

Visit **http://resident360.com/community** to check it out.

I'll see you there.

CHAPTER 4

HOW TO IMPROVE RESIDENT EXPERIENCE

The best customer is the one you already have, your resident. There are several strategies you can implement that will immediately improve resident experience. The first one I'm covering is a resident touchpoint plan.

RESIDENT TOUCHPOINT PLAN

This means each resident will be touched a certain amount of times throughout the life of their lease. Touching is nothing more than interaction with the resident.

The goal of the touchpoint plan is to show you care about their experience at your community.

See if you can create a twelve-month touchpoint plan or a touch for every month of the lease.

Here are some ideas:

- Housewarming gift
- After the first month, a move-in survey
- Rewards program
- Birthday cards (get creative)
- Handwritten thank-you note from Manager halfway through the lease
- Survey resident three months before the lease is up for renewal
- Lease renewal pizza party to discuss renewal in person

At the end of the day, you really have to create an experience that's above and beyond the resident's expectation.

What else can you do?

Here are some questions to ask yourself. How many can you answer yes to?

- Are service requests responded to in twenty-four hours or less?
- Is the community in tip-top shape?
- Do staff members go out of their way to help residents?
- Is the fitness center clean with updated equipment?
- Is the landscaping manicured?

- Are public areas like the pool and laundry room well kept?
- Do you have community events that bring residents together?
- Do residents view the community as safe?

MAINTENANCE PERSONNEL RUN-INS

Your residents probably have more run-ins with maintenance personnel than they do with you. That's why it's important that maintenance team members understand their roles in customer service and more importantly be on top of their game.

Here are four tips to help:

#1 Outward Appearance - Perception is reality. I don't care how smart the guy is, if he looks sloppy, that's how residents will see him as well. Make your maintenance staff look professional. What's your dress code? Company shirts?

#2 Appliance Use Videos - Most residents aren't reading manuals on how to work the dishwasher, stove, or microwave for that matter. Create short, mobile friendly videos featuring your onsite maintenance tech. These videos can properly demonstrate how to operate an appliance or answer a common question.

#3 Bring Gifts - Arm your maintenance techs with gifts to hand out to residents after a service call is done. For example, a maintenance tech fixes a toilet with a plunger. He can gift the plunger to the resident after the work is completed. Sounds funny, but why not.

#4 Surveys - The most important piece of all of this is the survey. As soon as a service request is completed, the resident needs to be surveyed on the service.

This is where most companies drop the ball. They don't make it easy for residents to give feedback.

All you need to ask is, "How was your service - Poor, Fair, Good." That's how simple it can be. If a resident says poor or fair, this should be an immediate indicator to you something wasn't right.

RESIDENT MOBILE APPS

Make it more convenient for your residents and get a mobile app for your community. The right app will allow your residents to submit service requests and pay rent right from their phone.

For example, at Resident360, we created the Resident Express Mobile App. Residents can download it from the Apple or Google Play Store. They can submit service requests, pay rent, view community news, refer friends, and even receive push notifications from onsite staff. The app makes communication between staff and residents easy.

If you can make life easier for your residents by implementing a community app, then it's something worth considering.

The Personal Touch

Another strategy is allowing residents to add personal design touches to their units to make the space more their own. This can be done at very little to no cost to you.

Changes can be as simple as:

- Wall color
- Light fixtures
- Adding a ceiling fan
- Flooring

In wrapping up this chapter, keep this in mind: Simple things do matter. Just remembering a resident's name, as well as the names of their children and pets, can make a big difference in their overall experience at your community.

CHAPTER 5

TIPS FOR GETTING A NEW WEBSITE

When viewing a website, it takes users less than two-tenths of a second to form a first impression, according to eye-tracking research conducted at Missouri University of Science and Technology.

In short, your website has an immediate impact and either attracts or repels prospective residents as soon as they land on it.

That's why this chapter is valuable. You'll get the questions you need to be asking your next website provider and you'll get tips for producing a great website.

Before you embark on getting a new website(s), you need to be thinking about how it will integrate with the property management software and third party services you're using.

For example:

Service requests - how would you like these handled on your new website? Should the website provider link to a resident portal? Would you rather have an email form on the website for service requests? Should the form actually integrate with your property management software? Or is this not important to you?

Online rent payment - do you have a rent payment provider in place like Rentpayment.com for this? Or is this being offered currently through your property management software provider?

Online leasing - do you plan on offering online leasing? Do you have a vendor in place who handles that for you now? Or do you prefer to just have an online or electronic application? Or should the provider build an online application for you?

Availability - how do you want unit availability handled on your new website? Would you like the website to integrate with your property management software, pull down available units, and show them on the website? Maybe this isn't important to you and you'd rather show a list of floor plan types with rent ranges.

TEN QUESTIONS YOU SHOULD BE ASKING

Now, let's take a look at the questions you should be asking before you invest in a new website.

These questions will help you:

Save time, <u>save money</u>, and ensure you make the right decision when choosing a website provider.

#1 – What's your process for delivering a new website?

This is usually the question most people forget to ask.

You don't want to be left with a massive headache and a six-month timeline for getting a new website, but it does happen if you choose the wrong website provider.

At my company Resident360, we have a four-step process for delivering a new website we call the 4D's - Discovery, Design, Develop, and Deploy. We give the client a document outlining this process, so they have a good understanding of what's required of them and when the website will be launched.

#2 - What's the price?

There are a number of factors that influence the price of a website, but expect to pay somewhere between $199 - $399 monthly for a good community website. Some of the factors that affect price are the following:

Integrations - will you be integrating any part of the website with property management software?

Photos - are you upgrading photographs of the community?

Floor plans - are you upgrading your floor plans from 2D to something like 3D?

Custom Design vs. Template - do you require a one hundred percent custom designed website or are you fine with a template design the company currently is offering?

> **PRO TIP**: Most companies will also offer volume discounting if you need websites for multiple properties.

#3 – What's unique about your websites?

This is a great question that will help you decide who to work with if you're looking at several website providers and you're not sure how to set them apart.

Keep in mind, it's not about having a hundred different features at a cheap price.

It's about having a great looking site designed specifically around your needs that generates leads without hassle to you.

#4 – Who is responsible for providing community photos?

When it comes to an apartment website, a picture is worth more than a thousand words. It's worth a thousand leads and leases.

Make sure to ask your website provider if they will provide a photographer to take new photos of your community.

It's hard to create a good-looking website with low-quality photos.

Most times having new photos taken will be an added cost, but even if it is, I suggest letting your website provider handle it because it can be a big hassle to manage the actual photographer.

The website provider will know exactly what shots to get, taking the guesswork away from you.

It also takes you out of the equation as the middleman having to coordinate file sizes and file access for the website provider.

#5 – Are your websites responsive?

Every website provider needs to be using Responsive Web Design. This means you have one website that automatically resizes and adjusts to fit whatever device a person is on – desktop, tablet, or Smartphone. This way you never lose a prospect due to the device they are on.

#6 – Are your websites SEO friendly and what does that include?

There are so many gray areas with "SEO friendly" websites and SEO strategies are always shifting and changing to adjust to the newest Google algorithm update.

With that said, I want to make sure you're educated so you know exactly what you're looking for.

An SEO friendly website or Search Engine Optimized Website is set up and coded properly so it gives itself the best chance at ranking in the search engines like Google, Yahoo, and Bing.

Every website provider has their own definition of what an SEO friendly website should include, but let me tell you the most important parts:

- Properly written title tags, meta descriptions, and H1 tags
- Properly written home page content
- Speed: fast loading website
- Good linking structure

#7 – Who is responsible for maintaining the website? Can I update it myself?

This can also be somewhat of a gray area and maintain can mean many different things.

In most cases, your website provider will be the one doing the real maintenance. That means if you ever have any security issues, like hacking or spamming, your website provider will handle resolving this. If you need basic changes, your website provider will handle this.

On the other hand, you will definitely want access to change things yourself, like rents and specials. Your on-site staff should be responsible for keeping that sort of content maintained.

#8 – Do you offer a resident portal?

A resident portal is a place on your website designed specifically for your residents. Typically, this includes an area to submit service requests and pay rent.

You'll find most property management software companies offer a resident portal as part of their offering. In other words, you may already have one. If this is the case for you, then chances are the company providing your new website will just link to this portal.

#9 – Who is hosting my website and what about backups?

This is also a very important question, even if it's on the technical, behind-the-scenes side of things.

You'll want to make sure your website is on a dedicated server with daily offsite backups and twenty-four/seven monitoring. This will give you peace of mind that your website will be up and running ninety-nine percent of the time.

#10 – What type of tracking and analytics do you offer?

Some website providers offer lead tracking solutions that include call tracking numbers/emails with reporting. At the very least, you want to understand your website traffic and where it's coming from. Having a reporting dashboard or weekly report emailed to you is essential.

~ ~ ~

Let's jump into some simple strategies and ideas for improving the look and response on new and existing community websites.

#1 - Showcase your reviews.

Create a "Resident Review" page on your website. This page will help combat any negative reviews floating around on other sites like apartmentratings.com. It will also serve as a convincing tool for visitors to your website. I talk more in depth about this strategy in Chapter 7.

#2 - Include Google Earth for showing distance.

We had a client who wanted to show how close their building was to the ocean. By utilizing Google Earth, we were able to zoom in and grab really unique looking imagery that captured the distance quite well. Can you do this for your own community?

#3 - Go big on your Pay Rent button.

If you accept online rent payments (which you should), make sure that button is highly visible on your website. Ideally, it should be in the top right hand side of your website and on every page. This takes the question out of the prospects mind, "Can I pay rent online at this community?"

#4 - Add a lifestyle video.

If you have a luxury property with high rents then it's worth investing in a quality video. Roughly costing around $15,000 you can show off the lifestyle aspect of your luxury community, models included. Even better to add the drone aspect to give the video a unique look and feel.

#5 - Use video backgrounds.

I personally love when I come to a website and they have a video playing in the background. It's something unique and not many communities are utilizing this effect in multifamily. It can easily elevate the look and feel of your website. Just be careful with the load time of your website.

#6 - Increase cool factor with weather widgets, surf report, etc.

If you have a coastal apartment community why not add the surf report to your website? Is your apartment community in the mountains? Add the ski report. Do you just want to show the weather? You can do that as well.

There are website widgets available for all these and more. This is a simple way to make your website appear fresh and updated.

#7 - Add a Special Offer opt-in form.

Do you run specials? Why not push these out through a type of pop-up form, where the visitor has to put in their email address to get it. Now you have a way to market back to this person. Plus, you know they're interested as they just gave you their email for your special offer.

There are several tools for adding this to your website. Sumome.com and Optinmonster.com offer the most variety of website pop-ups and are inexpensive.

#8 - Add live chat.

This is a super, simple way to engage website visitors immediately. I'm surprised more companies aren't using it.

I prefer Olark.com, as their live chat tool is easy to install and you can turn it on and off whenever you want. They have a free and paid version. We use the free version at Resident360.com.

#9 - Increase your phone number size.

Put your phone number at the top of every page on your website. Make sure it stands out. You'd be surprised at how many website providers don't do this for their clients. Does yours?

#10 - Use "you" more than "we."

Use the word "you" and you'll speak directly to your prospects. Rely on the word "we" and they'll switch off and go elsewhere. Talk about your customer, not yourself—you can't bore someone into leasing from you.

#11 - Use short sentences.

People's attention spans are getting shorter —and some say they weren't too long to begin with. If you want prospects to turn into actual leads, get your point across before they have a chance to nod off.

#12 - Break up your text.

Use short paragraphs, lists, pictures, quotes, subheadings, and boxes to give your website variety. If you do, people will read what you have to say.

#13 - Ask for the lead.

It's as simple as adding "call to actions" next to the areas where customers can contact you. If you have a phone number add, "Call now to check availability" next to it. The same thing goes for email forms. "Fill out this form to check availability."

#14 - Cross-promote other properties.

Anytime a prospect fills out a contact form on your website, have the Thank-You page they see after clicking "Submit" to promote your other properties and their websites.

#15 - Photo the heck out of it.

This is the best investment you can make for your website. Look for a photographer who specializes in Real Estate. Create a shot list, pick a nice, sunny day, and make sure the common areas are clean.

Do you have a luxury property? Bring in models to show off your properties best assets. Don't forget, you can use these photos in all your marketing. Here's an idea: ask a few residents to become part of the photo shoot. Get action shots of people diving into your pool or real life shots of dogs playing in your pet park.

#16 - Make over your rates and floor plans page.

When visitors come to your website they want to know three things—location, cost, and what the floor plans look like. Spending the extra time making over your rates and floor plans page is something you need to do. Crisp, clear floor plans, a nice page layout, and clearly illustrated pricing will help the website visitor experience and probably result in more leads. How do your rates and floor plans pages look?

We have many clients at Resident360 who are upgrading their 2D floor plans to 3D or plans. This is one of the easiest upgrades you can make. I think giving the website visitor the option to view both is ideal.

#17 - Create a Content model.

Add a blog to your apartment website. Update it monthly with fun things that are happening either at your community or in your area. Then syndicate these blog posts on your social media profiles to help create more social links pointing back to your website. Prospects love it, residents love it, and it will help you rank better on search engines.

#18 - Get creative with your fonts.

Website fonts are one of the most underutilized marketing tools out there for multifamily. Experiment with two to three different font styles for your website to make your text come alive. It's one of the easy things you can do to improve the look of any website.

I'm a fan of handwriting fonts, as well as big and bold ones. Some of my favorites are Manus and Dancing Script. Good places to search for fonts are dafont.com and google.com/fonts.

WRAPPING UP AND WHAT YOU SHOULD DO NEXT

Your website should be your number one source of leads, your communication hub, and the center for all your marketing. Spending the time in advance to think through what you want, asking the right questions, and implementing some of the tips above will help you achieve this.

Want the Latest in Apartment Marketing?

There's a great deal of information covered in this book and many of these topics are discussed in depth in my weekly e-newsletter.

Join the community of over 4,000 multifamily professionals and get tips, tactics, and tutorials delivered to your inbox every Wednesday.

Visit **http://resident360.com/community** to check it out.

I'll see you there.

CHAPTER 6

HOW TO GET TRAFFIC TO YOUR WEBSITE

Now that you have the foundation of what makes a great community website and the questions you should be asking, the next thing is obviously to drive traffic to your site. In this chapter, we are going to look at:

- The different types of traffic and where it comes from

- Using Google to drive traffic

- Keywords explained

- Using backlinks to get traffic

- Using citations to get traffic

- Google Analytics and traffic analysis

TRAFFIC AND WHERE IT COMES FROM

There are many ways to get traffic to your community website, but let's first break down the different types of website traffic so you have a better understanding.

I also want to add a quick disclaimer. I talk quite a bit about Google throughout this chapter and in many of the other chapters in this book. Just be aware, Yahoo, Bing, and other search engines do exist out there. However, at the time of writing this book, Google has the majority of search engine traffic so I'm focusing exclusively on them.

There are four types of traffic you need to be aware of:

- Direct Traffic - when someone types your website address directly into their browser.

- Paid Traffic - when someone arrives at your website via a paid advertisement.

- Organic Traffic - when someone arrives at your website by using a search engine like Google, Yahoo, or Bing.

- Referral Traffic when someone arrives at your website by clicking on a direct link from another website.

4 Types of Website Traffic

Let's look at all the different traffic sources that can send people to your website. This is by no means a complete list, but should give you a good overview:

- Referrals - People hear about your community and can Google your community name or type your website directly into a browser.

- Friends - Friends hear about your community and can Google your community name or type your website directly into a browser.

- Print Advertising - People see your advertisement and either Google your community name or type your website directly into a browser.

- Videos - People see a video and either Google your community name, click a direct link in the video description, or type your website directly into a browser.

- Google Adwords (Pay Per Click) - People click an ad in Google search results and arrive at your website via paid advertising.

- Craigslist - People see an ad for your community and either Google your community name or type your website directly into a browser.

- Social Media - People see a post or an ad with a direct link to your website or Google your community name or type your website directly into a browser.

- Drive by - People see your massive sign as they drive by your community and either Google your community name or type your website directly into a browser.

- Internet Listing Services - People either Google your community name or type your website directly into a browser or direct link to your website depending on the ILS.

- Email Marketing - People click a direct link to your website after you send them an email.

- Search Engines - People search keywords, including your community name, and arrive at your website via a search result.

- Content Marketing - People find articles, photos, videos, infographics, and even audio about your community that's engaging, and typically click a direct link to your website or Google your community name.

This list alone should give you a real understanding of how important it is to have a great website representing your community. Not just a great website, but one that is fully responsive, so it works properly on all devices—desktop, tablet, and mobile.

You don't want to be turning away people who drive by your community and have their phone out Googling your community name. Give them a great mobile experience so you can capture the lead.

Now that you're familiar with the different types of traffic and sources, let's discuss in detail what your community website needs to attract more traffic.

USING GOOGLE TO DRIVE TRAFFIC

At Resident360, we work with lots of communities that want their website to be ranked on the first page of Google. This requires several components and strategies and can take months before you start seeing results.

In other words, it isn't something that magically happens overnight. My goal here is to lay down the basics so, at least, you have a good understanding of what Google is looking for when they rank websites on the first page of results.

First, a quick disclaimer; no one knows, including me, what Google really wants or is looking for. Their algorithm, or how they rank websites, is top secret. What we have, though, is years of knowledge and trends and my own personal experience of ranking websites for over twelve years now.

What does Google look for in ranking a website?

- Good website design
- Aged website domain
- Great fresh content updated frequently
- Website visitors and returning visitors
- Fast loading website
- Low bounce rates
- High time on website
- Good website coding
- Relevant quality backlinks
- Keywords, but not too many
- …and a whole lot more stuff…

The big thing you need to remember is Google loves websites that have great content. Great content brings readers, encourages sharing on social media, and brings more relevant high-quality backlinks to the website. (A backlink is nothing more than a direct link back to your website from another website.)

How does a community website fit into this? Well, having a content strategy can really help your website rank better on the search engines.

At my company, Resident360, we have resident blogs as part of our community websites. These blogs are updated weekly with good content that comes directly from the community. It keeps residents informed and coming to the website and it helps prospects get a fresh look at living in that community. It's a win-win.

In addition to great content, you have to have a well-designed and programmed website. Unfortunately, most of us don't know what's under the hood of our websites. Yes, we can see the design and it may look nice, but that really means nothing. It comes down to the actual programming and coding.

The best way for you to get a slight peek under the hood of your website is to use two tools from Google. Google Analytics and Google Search Console. They're fairly simple to add your website and each has its own unique set of traits.

Google Analytics measures—you guessed it—analytics. What's important here is it gives you the average time people are spending on your website, the bounce rate, and page load times. If you have an average time on site above two minutes, a bounce rate below fifty percent, and a page load time of less than five seconds, you're doing pretty well. I'll go into much more detail on Google Analytics shortly.

Google Search Console helps measure the health of your website. It will give you details such as configuration issues, health issues, traffic, and even optimization help. I know it sounds kind of technical, but the big thing I pay attention to here are the errors that are found on my community websites, like crawl errors, broken links, and malware. Search Console lets me know what they are so I can get them fixed.

KEYWORDS EXPLAINED

If there's one thing I think many people have some understanding of, it's adding keywords to your website so you show up in Google search results. Yes, you want to have relevant keywords in different areas of your website.

This will help tell Google what words to rank you for in the search engines. Unfortunately, it's much more than just adding keywords to your website to show up in the search results, or at least on the first page.

Let's talk quickly about how you pick keywords for your website. There's a great tool to help you do this from Google called the Keyword Planner. If you Google it, it will more than likely be the first search result.

This tool allows you to put in any keyword you like, for example, Pacific Beach Apartments. Then what happens is it gives you the volume of how many people are searching that particular keyword on Google. Plus, it will give you different variations that people are searching for, like Pacific Beach San Diego Apartments.

Choosing good keywords is like a science. You can choose the keywords that have the most searches, keywords with middle of the road searches, or keywords that have the least amount of searches.

Keep in mind, the keywords with the most searches are also the most competitive. That means it may take much more time and hard work to reach the first page of Google search results.

One of our strategies here at Resident360, is to go after something called a long tail keyword. These are keyword phrases that have at least five words.

For example, a long tail keyword could be pet-friendly apartments in Cincinnati. We then create a separate page on our community websites directly focused on this particular long tail keyword.

This keyword is added to the URL of the page, the title tag, meta description, H1 tag (I'm coming to all these), and listed in the text on the page. We've found it fairly easy to rank quickly using this strategy.

That brings me to my next point. Where should these keywords be on your website? Not to sound redundant, but these keywords should be in your title tag, meta description, H1 tag, should appear in your text, and if possible also your page name or URL.

Let's dig deeper.

Title Tags, Meta Descriptions, and H1 Tags are among the most overlooked items on a community website. They may sound like foreign terms to you now, but you see them any time you do a Google search.

What you see is the title tag first (which is underlined) followed by the website link underneath, followed by a description (meta description) of the website.

When a prospect is searching for an apartment, this title tag and meta description is telling them what the website essentially is about. By including your keyword in both, it helps Google rank your website for that particular search term as well.

Unfortunately, most community websites don't take advantage of this. Most times you'll find the title tag and meta description without the keyword, with grammar issues, and poor phrases that really make no sense at all.

Ideally, you want to use this space as a mini sales message for your community. Remember, a prospect is searching Google for an apartment. Your website comes up in the search results. To give you the best shot at getting them to click your listing, you need to sell them on why you are their best choice.

Look at the two examples of a title tag and meta description below. Which one would you want to click on?

Example One:

> **Estancia Apartments** (Title Tag)
>
> Estancia apartments, scottsdale az, Homes, apartments, apartments for rent, community management company. (Meta Description)

Example Two:

> **Apartments Scottsdale | Estancia *Luxury Apartments* in Scottsdale, AZ** (Title Tag)
>
> Move in to a better life at *Estancia Apartments* in Scottsdale AZ. Stress free living is waiting for you. Pet friendly community. Click for more info. (Meta Description)

Obviously, example two is more exciting and speaks directly to the prospective resident.

As I said before, this is one of the most overlooked, easy things you can do to help your website get more traffic.

Finally, we have the **H1 tag**. The H1 tag is pretty much the main headline on each page of your website. The H1 tag tells Google what the actual website page is about. Therefore, if you have a headline on the home page of your website, you want to make sure it's set as an H1 tag (most aren't). You also want to make sure it has some variation of your keyword in the headline. For example:

"Brand New Luxury Apartments in Cincinnati"

The keyword phrase here is "Luxury Apartments in Cincinnati."

Just having the keyword in your headline and having it set as an H1 tag will help rank your website better.

USING BACKLINKS TO GET TRAFFIC

Now that we've addressed website structure let's talk about running quality backlinks to your website. A backlink is a direct incoming link to your website from another site that has what is called an anchor text or keyword attached to it.

For example, you're reading a story on CNN and you see a highlighted word. You click the highlighted word and it takes you to another website. This would be considered a backlink. The highlighted word would be considered the anchor text or keyword.

The story behind backlinks is that there was a time when the more backlinks you had pointing to your website the higher your site ranked in the search results for that specific keyword. That led to websites buying thousands of really low-quality, spammy backlinks. Eventually, Google caught on to this and changed their algorithm to penalize this sort of behavior.

What's important today is high-quality relevant backlinks. An example of this would be a popular apartment blog, a multifamily association like the NAA, or even a forum like Multifamily Insiders, that all link back to your website. This would help you rank better in the search results.

Even powerful news sites that link to your website can give you a big boost in search engine rankings.

Here's a quick story to reinforce this point:

I was writing on a personal business blog I own. The blog averages about 850 unique visitors a month. One day, the blog had a huge spike in unique visitors. Wondering what had happened, I logged on to Google Analytics and researched where the traffic was coming from. I found out *The New York Times* had mentioned my blog on their website. They even gave a backlink to the specific article on my blog they mentioned. This one backlink boosted the blog to the top of the search results for many competitive keywords. This resulted in an increase in monthly traffic.

The moral of this story is you don't need lots of backlinks. You simply need a few high-quality ones. I'm still shocked about being mentioned in *The New York Times*. How cool is that?

USING CITATIONS TO GET TRAFFIC

This is a great time to segue into the next thing I want to discuss—citations. Citations help improve your local search engine rankings. A citation is a business listing in a large or even small niche directory. For example, Yelp.com, Apartments.com, and Forrent.com are considered directories.

The listing includes your community name, address, phone number, and other relevant information. Oftentimes, citations will also include backlinks to your website.

What's great about citations are even though you may not get a backlink to your website, just the mention of your community, with exact matching data (name, address, and phone number—aka NAP), will help your website rank better.

The strategy behind citations is you want to have more than one referencing your community. The more you can get the better.

Here's a list of places to get citations:

- ✓ ILS - apartments.com, forrent.com
- ✓ Yelp - yelp.com
- ✓ Superpages - superpages.com
- ✓ City Search - citysearch.com
- ✓ Express Update USA - expressupdateusa.com
- ✓ Yahoo Local - local.yahoo.com
- ✓ Insider Pages - insiderpages.com

GOOGLE ANALYTICS AND TRAFFIC ANALYSIS

The final piece tying everything together is Google Analytics, an insightful website traffic analytic tool. It's easy to add to your website and the information it gives you about your website traffic is pure gold.

Google Analytics has become pretty complex over the last few years in terms of everything you can do with it. Here's an overview of what to pay attention to:

- Users - how many people are visiting your website?

- Page Views - what's the average number of pages people are viewing?

- Average Session Duration - what's the average amount of time visitors are spending on the website?

- Bounce Rate - are visitors leaving after landing on your home page or are they digging deeper into the website? Simply put, you want a bounce rate under fifty percent.

- Mobile - how many visits do you have from mobile devices and how long are they staying on the site?

- Acquisition/Overview - what are the top five traffic sources sending people to your website?

- Keywords - what are the top ten keywords people are searching on a search engine that put them on your website?

By having Google Analytics in place, it was easy for me to research and find *The New York Times* article linking to my blog post. I looked under "Referrals" and saw the exact URL that mentioned my blog post. I could also see how many people clicked over from the mention.

It's a great tool and I can't recommend it enough. Now, you probably have Google Analytics in place on your current community website, but my guess is you have never logged in and looked at a report.

Make sure you set some time aside to do this. You should always be aware of what's happening on your website in terms of traffic. It's a key ingredient to generating high-quality leads from your website.

CHAPTER 7

HOW TO MANAGE YOUR REPUTATION

Negative reviews on apartmentratings.com, Yelp, and Google Places can ruin more than just your ego. The last thing you want a prospective resident to see is the first line of a negative Google review when they click on your location on a Google Map. Especially when it's something like: *"DoN't ReNt hErE!!!! It sUX."*

Although you can't do much about former residents who think they should receive their entire deposit back, even though their cat peed on every available surface in the apartment, you can make a difference for reasonable residents by simply giving them more information so they have healthy expectations about the resident experience and the move-out experience.

I have found the most common complaints on apartment ratings sites are issues that really boil down to a resident's expectations.

> PLEASE DON'T MOVE IN HERE!
> They give you nothing but headaches.
> They are lazy, they don't care, they have attitudes.
> Worst place I've ever lived in.
> Nothing about this place is special.
> I'm going to report and if I can, I'm going to sue this place.
> That's how much I'm tired of it.
> There are so many apartments waaaaaaaaay better than this.
> DON'T MOVE IN! You'll regret it!

If you (or your leasing agents) take the time to train and educate your residents about how things work at your community when they sign the lease, it can change everything.

Some key topics that need to be discussed during the move-in lease signing include:

- How your after-hours emergency maintenance reporting system works.

- How you will communicate with a resident in case of a building-wide (or unit-specific) emergency.

- How and where to submit maintenance requests and what kind of response to expect (phone call, maintenance man just shows up, etc.)

- How to submit a thirty-day notice when they are ready to move out and what kind of confirmation they can expect in order to be certain their notice was processed.

Another important time to manage expectations (and therefore reduce ex-resident disappointment) is when they put in a thirty-day Move-Out notice. It is crucial they understand how your move-out process works, when they can expect their refund, and what types of things they can expect to be charged for.

The place where your efforts are most meaningful is face-to-face with the resident. If you want to boost your apartmentratings.com reviews, offer amazing customer service so residents receive clear communication and never even bother to go vent their frustration online. Although, there are of course, many unreasonable people in the world, most residents only end up being frustrated when their expectations were not met. Communicating clearly, so the resident understands your systems and processes, not only protects your community from those damaging negative Google or apartmentratings.com reviews, it also boosts the positive word of mouth comments from previous residents.

Help your staff create a culture of clear communication with residents so there is less confusion during the term of the lease and after move-out. This will help you reduce the kind of frustration and anger that leads someone to post a negative review full of complaints on apartmentratings.com. Customer service and clear communication go a long way toward resident retention and resident referrals.

ADDRESSING NEGATIVE REVIEWS

If you receive a negative review, don't panic. Take the time to think out your response and always be positive. You want to respond as a real human being with good intentions. The goal of the response is to show you actually care.

Here's an example of a manager responding to a negative review on apartmentratings.com:

> I really appreciate your taking the time to give us some insight into your thoughts about the community. We are exploring some options into new changes for the inside of the homes I think you will like. As for your neighbors and the dog, I'm more than happy to address the noise if you contact me offline so we can figure out where it's coming from. As for the dog, we have some homes here that have been approved for larger dogs in accordance with the Americans with Disabilities Act. While I cannot say this is the case for the dog that lived above you, I can certainly look into the matter privately. Give me a call at (XXX) XXX-XXXX, email me at xxxx@gmail.com or stop by the office during the week so we can talk more. Look forward to hearing from you.

It may not be perfect, but it goes a long way for prospective residents researching your community and coming across these reviews. The danger lies in not saying anything at all.

The second part of responding to negative reviews is social proof. Get your existing residents to give you positive reviews on these sites to help bury the negative ones.

I think we both know this is not easily done, as a resident has to go out of their way to log on to a website like apartmentratings.com or Google Places to give the review. What I found to work well is to ask and make it easy for them to give the review.

That's right, just ask residents who you know are having a good experience living in your community. Then make it easy for them to give the positive review by emailing them a link directly to the site. Simple stuff, right?

Well, it is that simple—you just have to follow through. Here's an example of this in action. At Resident360, we recently emailed a large number of residents at a few properties. This was a big email blast that asked the residents to give us a review (good or bad) on apartmentratings.com.

The email included a link to the apartmentratings.com page for that particular community. This email went out over one day. Within twenty-four hours, we had over fifty new reviews on apartmentratings.com. Not knowing what to expect, we were pleasantly surprised to see that an overwhelming number of the reviews were positive. This helped raise our rating for the particular communities on apartmentratings.com.

Now, I don't recommend incentivizing for good reviews as this can backfire on you. The last thing you want is a resident posting a negative review saying they were given a Starbucks gift card as an incentive.

Another good way to add social proof to your community is to have lots of genuine testimonials on your website, and on all your marketing for that matter.

The absolute best time to get a testimonial is right after you give the residents their keys when moving in. Think about it. They made a financial decision. They chose your community. They feel good about the decision they made. This is the testimonial sweet spot.

When you hand them their keys and they say thank-you, follow-up with, "Would you mind giving us a quick testimonial as to why you chose our community?" Rarely will you hear no.

The next question going through your mind might be what type of questions to ask them. It's important to keep it simple. If a resident is just moving in, you can ask them, "Why did you choose to lease here?" The answer to that one question alone might be all you need for a good testimonial.

IT'S IMPORTANT TO TAKE CARE
OF YOUR CUSTOMERS!

What else can be done to further enhance your apartment community's online reputation?

When asking this question, it seems the common denominator in every answer is managing your presence on someone else's platform, i.e. apartmentratings.com, Yelp, etc.

What if we flipped this whole thing upside down and looked at it from a completely different perspective?

Instead of taking the approach of just managing what others are saying about you on all these other third party websites, why not create your own apartment reviews page that presents happy, satisfied residents instead of the few frustrated ones.

This would give your community a real upper hand, making it easy for prospects to see the positive and completely eliminate the negative.

Creating your own apartment reviews website page is not as hard as it may sound. The basic steps are either add a page designated for reviews to your existing website, or create a new stand-alone website landing page for this purpose.

Here's the basic outline of how to do it:

1. Create a Review Page on your community website.

2. Make sure the On-Page SEO of this page is properly done. That means using your keyword such as,

"Estancia Apartments Resident Reviews" in the title tag, meta description, H1 tag, URL, and text of the page.

(You want this page to rank when people search your community name + reviews. The goal is to outrank apartmentratings.com and Yelp)

3. Create three to five fun signs about your community. Basically, positive statements like:

- I love living at [Your Community]
- Happy Resident
- The Leasing Staff is Awesome
- Pet Friendly
- Walking Distance to [Area]
- I Love The [Community Name] Staff

4. Ask residents to hold the sign and snap a photo of them.

5. Upload the photo to your review page.

6. Rinse and repeat the process.

Why I Love This Strategy

Yes—it's all one-sided, positive reviews about your community, but who cares. What I really like is you're capturing the demographic of your community in a visual way and posting it for all prospects to see.

It answers the question, "Who lives here?" Now the prospective resident can see photos of people they can relate to.

Recycling Your Social Proof

Here's a great tip for building consistent social proof over multiple review and social sites. Take your reviews and share them from one review site to another.

In other words, recycle them...

If you have a positive comment on your Facebook page, take a screenshot of the comment and share it on your ILS page like ApartmentFinder.com.

Maybe you have pictures of residents holding positive signs about your community (like previously mentioned). Make sure to upload these to your Facebook page and your review sites.

The goal here is to recycle the social proof. Just because it's on one site, doesn't mean you can't use it on all sites.

Let me wrap up this chapter by stating the obvious. You have to be proactive and put a plan in place for handling reviews, social proof, and testimonials. You can't just sit on the sideline and hope for the best.

It all starts with realizing your best customer is your existing resident. Provide a quality living experience for them and you'll more than likely benefit with positive reviews, testimonials, leads, referrals, and renewals. They can be your best, unpaid sales force.

Want the Latest in Apartment Marketing?

There's a great deal of information covered in this book and many of these topics are discussed in depth in my weekly e-newsletter.

Join the community of over 4,000 multifamily professionals and get tips, tactics, and tutorials delivered to your inbox every Wednesday.

Visit **http://resident360.com/community** to check it out.

I'll see you there.

CHAPTER 8

HOW TO WORK SMARTER

There are many big, long-term things you can do to impact your marketing, but there are also small fixes and habit changes that can positively impact your effectiveness. Implement these five things today and it can increase your productivity, traffic to your website, and streamline your workflow.

1) Always reread your emails before you click send.

This seems basic, but most people don't do it. It may take an extra few seconds to skim and reread, but it's faster than having to undo a miscommunication. Whether you are interacting with a resident, a prospect, or a manager above you, it's important to communicate clearly, simply—and ideally with as few errors as possible. Of course, some minor spelling errors can be overlooked, but sometimes a small typo can change the meaning, so take one minute and reread before you send.

2) Put your community web address in your email signature.

Again, this seems basic, but unfortunately, it's often overlooked. Whether you are communicating with prospects or current residents, your website should have content that is valuable for both. Always make it as easy as possible for people to get to your website and share your website.

3) Use "if/then" statements.

This is another way to communicate clearly and offer specific action steps for the recipient. This is a great tip I heard about from Tim Ferris, author of *The 4-Hour Work Week*. My work week is still over forty hours, but this little tip has helped me use email more effectively. Here are some examples of how you could use if/then statements in emails:

To a prospect: "Are you available to schedule a tour for Friday at 3:00 p.m.? If not, let me know a specific time that would work for you during the hours of 9:00 a.m. - 6:00 p.m."

To a co-worker or regional manager: "Do you have the new photos from the photographer? If not, when can we expect them?"

To a resident: "Thanks for asking about our pet policy before you adopted a new cat. If you are going to get a pet, then you'll need to fill out our pet policy addendum. If you stop by the office on Saturday, I can give you a copy."

4) Keep your message focused.

Big blocks of text are hard to read or digest easily. Again, whether you are communicating with residents, prospects, or internally with someone you manage or who manages you, keep the point of your message clear.

Make the subject line specific to the information or action needed. Use bullet points whenever possible. Add space between paragraphs.

Don't use vague phrases that will require the recipient to email you and ask more questions before they can take action.

For example, saying, "the washing machine isn't working," doesn't give enough information. That ends up requiring another round of emails back and forth to understand the specifics of what isn't working, what happened when you tried it, and what you need to solve the problem.

5) Take action and organize next steps.

When you open an email, have a system ready to make a list of actions you need to take. Whether it's digital or just paper and pen, be ready to organize and keep track of things you need to do based on your emails. If it makes sense for your responsibilities, make separate lists based on the type of action.

For example, list all vendor related actions in one column, all actions to delegate in another column, and resident related actions in another column, etc. You may want to order your tasks by priority or deadlines.

Approach your inbox as a task list, instead of a chaotic monster. Reply immediately if you can, and if not, write down a clear action you need to take to be able to follow-up or complete a request.

Don't just write: "pest control #111." Instead, write: "Call to schedule pest control for Tuesday. Unit #111."

This will help you reduce the chaos in your office and help you stay on top of resident requests. When residents have their needs met and don't have to keep bothering you until something gets done, they stay happier and they stay in your community.

Using email effectively and improving your communication skills is good for your career, can reduce wasted time, and can make it easier for you and your staff to work together and serve your residents.

Implement these simple tips today and experience immediate improvements in your productivity and workflow, while also possibly drawing more traffic to your website. It's a win-win all around.

Let's move on to the topic of learning.

If you're one of the few professionals who feel like they have a manageable workload and your inbox is always at zero, then high five to you. However, I think it's more common that people generally feel the opposite. The challenge is to prioritize, put out fires, but also make sure you stay on top of the important stuff, not just the urgent stuff.

No matter how busy you are, it's pivotal to keep learning and stay inspired. Continuing to grow and learn will not only increase your value to the company you work for, but it can also improve your satisfaction and enjoyment of the job.

So, how can you fit one more thing you *should* do into your schedule? "Not enough time," is usually the biggest objection to any positive change.

First, it starts with believing the habit has value and then pay attention to the positive benefits once you do it. When you start seeing the impact, it will be much easier to continue even when it's not convenient.

Here are ten ideas for busy multifamily professionals to keep learning and stay inspired:

1. Integrate exercise with learning by listening to a business, apartment industry, or personal growth audio book while you jog or take a leisurely walk in the evening after dinner.

2. Take initiative to be the expert at your community on the newest technology tool you're using. Whether it's the back-end of your website, the dashboard for your lead tracking, or mobile app. Learn everything you can about it so you are the go-to person who understands the tool and can leverage it at your community.

3. Ask a peer to have lunch or coffee with you every week or every other week so you can each share what you've been learning. Plan to discuss things that went well for you and areas where you are working to improve. It can really make a difference to have a safe place to just share and process, especially when it comes to your leasing strategies. Hold each other accountable to continue growing and practice communicating what you're absorbing.

4. Choose one topic to learn about each month. Even if you don't make it a weekly or daily habit, you'll at least be working on your own development with a structure that can keep you engaged. Small progress is still progress.

5. Write down your career goals for the year and select specific areas you want to learn more about. Make a

plan for how you will spend time investing in your own learning and career off the clock. When you have a goal, it's easier to invest in learning and growing because you specifically see where it's going.

6. Next time you're watching a required training, certification class, make a note of two to three specific things mentioned that you want to learn more about. If there was a word mentioned you're not familiar with, or a resource that seemed interesting, write it down. Then, Google the topic and read more than one article on the subject. I always recommend reading more than one article on any given topic because there are so many different viewpoints on the internet.

7. Listen to a podcast on your commute, or even at home in the morning while you get dressed and ready.

8. If you've been especially bogged down by negative reviews or complaining residents, be sure to spend your commute or lunch break focusing on positive things. Find ways to laugh and reset your focus, instead of just venting or complaining. Be intentional to get some perspective and not take it personally. Spending five minutes like this can transform your day and your attitude.

9. Get to work ten minutes early and spend that short time reading an article on a blog or newspaper about marketing, maintenance, leasing, or anything that will

motivate you to work smart that day. Alternatively, spend ten minutes of your lunch break reading something that will pump you up with energy and motivation to stay focused.

10. Ask your manager, regional manager, or marketing director for their suggestions about how you can grow your career. Ask for feedback about the areas they see you have the potential to grow in. Ask for their ideas about specific opportunities to learn so you can go above and beyond.

There's no end to the ways you can take responsibility for your career and your attitude at work. Of course, the challenge is just doing it. I believe if you make the small shifts, you'll begin to experience the benefits that will keep you inspired and motivated to do more.

CHAPTER 9

A FINAL THOUGHT

I want to congratulate you on making it all the way through this comprehensive guide on apartment marketing. I hope you learned some great takeaways and strategies you can put in place.

Just remember, when it comes to marketing, you have many options. I can't sit here and say one thing will work better than the next for your community. Every community, city, and demographic is different. What may work for one may not work so well for the next.

The key is to test, test, and test some more. Try different things and make sure you keep accountability in place so you know what's working and what's not. That's how you market effectively. Do more of the things that work and less of the things that don't. Never rely on just one source for leads as well. Diversify your marketing by having an online and offline strategy aimed at generating traffic, leads, and engaging residents.

Think about your digital footprint as well and how you can continually build on it. Some of the Internet marketing sources and strategies laid out in this book can help you. It's important as we move more into the digital age and you'll benefit by reaching prospects in different ways you've never even thought about.

To conclude, it's important to remember your best customer is the one you already have—your existing residents. Make sure any marketing plan you put in place involves them, as they can be your best sales force.

Thanks so much for allowing me to walk you through this information. I hope you've learned a great deal and I can't wait to hear your feedback.

CHAPTER 10

FREQUENTLY ASKED QUESTIONS

Although the answers to many of these questions are actually in the book, I thought it helpful to highlight them here as well. You can refer back to the earlier chapters to get further insight.

If I had to pick one strategy for apartment marketing, what would it be?

Assuming you have a good converting community website, I would use Google Adwords to drive traffic to your website. With Adwords, you can target people searching on Google for an apartment and you can remarket to them if they've gone to your website and left. You can also implement Geo-Targeting around your community for driving very cheap traffic. With Adwords, you control the budget and all traffic goes to your website.

Is it really important to have a good community website?

Yes, your community website should be the hub of all your marketing. Additionally, it should be your number one source for leads and leases. Another way to look at it is, what happens when a prospective resident Googles your community name? Does your community website show up? If so, what first impression is it going to make on the prospect? This is happening as we speak. That's why you have to have a community website that makes a good first impression and is set up for converting the prospect into a lead.

How much does it cost for a good community website?

That's really an open-ended question because it depends on your goals and what you want that community website to accomplish. On average, expect to spend $200 - $400 monthly for a good website.

I'm on a budget, what do you think is the best, least expensive thing I can do to get more leads?

I would use Craigslist. It's free; you just need to write good ads, have good photos, and post consistently.

How can I free up more time for marketing?

My recommendation is to time block. Block one hour a day to handle the marketing and nothing else. Depending on your role in the company, you'll need to figure out what time that is. It needs to be distraction free, so if that's turning off the cell phone and email, then do it. One hour of focused concentration on marketing. Otherwise, hire someone.

How long does it take to get ranked on the first page of Google?

Well, that depends on how competitive the keyword is you're trying to get ranked for. It also depends on how well your community website is set up to get ranked and if you have a search engine marketing strategy in place to help you get ranked. Assuming you have a very SEO friendly website, a competent search engine marketing strategy, and a non-competitive long tail keyword you want to rank for, it can happen as fast as a week to three months. Highly competitive words can take upward of six to twelve months. You never know what Google is going to do. They are constantly changing their ranking algorithm with updates, which can push you higher or in some cases lower in the search results. You have to be consistent and stick with your strategy.

What do you think is the most valuable lead source?

Your existing residents are your most valuable lead source. Treat them right and you'll get renewals and referrals. A resident referral costs you very little and the prospect is already sold before talking to you. Your community website would be the next most valuable.

What is a fully responsive website?

Wikipedia says it best—responsive web design, often abbreviated as RWD, is a web design approach aimed at crafting sites to provide an optimal viewing experience—easy reading and navigation with a minimum of resizing, panning, and scrolling—across a wide range of devices (from desktop computer monitors to mobile phones).

Is there an easy way to monitor what's being said about my community on the Internet?

You can use Google alerts. It's easy to set up, plus it's free. You want to make sure someone is actually looking at the emails Google sends that mention your community. Google isn't foolproof, so it's not a bad idea to have someone manually check apartmentratings.com and Yelp daily for mentions of your community.

What is the best way to schedule more community tours?

Listen to more leasing calls and see where improvements can be made. Have a better follow-up process in place that focuses on a tighter window of time and utilizes more than one method of follow-up.

What is the best way to get more resident renewals?

Improve the resident experience. Make sure work orders are completed within twenty-four hours and proper follow-up is put in place. Provide clean, safe, and friendly grounds. Make it an easy place to live. Give service that's above and beyond one hundred percent. Don't forget to smile and have a positive uplifting attitude—that in itself goes a long way.

CATCHY CRAIGSLIST AD TITLES

Your job is to sell the click first. That's right. You have to get the prospective resident to click your Craigslist ad title before they can see your ad.

Most apartment communities forget this and just slap any old title on their ad only to see very few results. Don't let that be you. Here's a comprehensive list of titles to help:

1. Lovely 2 Bedroom Apartment… Waiting for You to Make it Home!

2. Newly Renovated With Amazing Natural Light

3. Love this building! Love this location! Amazing Stuff in Cool Area

4. BRAND NEW LUX BLDG+wrap around balconies+loft unit+MUST SEE

5. UPDATED! GREAT AMENITIES! GREAT LOCATION! AMAZING APARTMENT UNITS!

6. Below Market Price! Awesome value! GREAT Location!

7. STYLISH STUDIO ~ 2-CAR PARKING, HUGE CLOSET, FIREPLACE, LAUNDRY

8. Charming Location near Main Street! Wood Floors! Pool!

9. RARELY AVAILABLE 2 BED, 2 BATH NEW APARTMENT

10. Do not look past this three bedroom in Lakeshore East!

11. ▶▶BRIGHT CORNER one bedroom on South Beach!

12. Quiet, Clean, and Peaceful. Very Nice RENOVATED efficiency.

13. Amazing Opportunity to Live in Downtown

14. ▶▶STUDIO IN GREAT AREA. NO COMMUTE! ◀◀

15. Affordable living! Wonderful floor plans for every budget!

16. ✂ Cut Down on Move-In Costs with $300 Off!!

17. Looking for A Bigger Place… Try Us

18. Start summer off in your new apartment home with POOL VIEW!

19. Looking For Convenience? Well, Look No Further!

20. You'll fall in LOVE with the VIEW! Rent Today! Convenient Location!

21. RARE VACANCY in this luxury apartment!

22. Cozy up to your wood-burning fireplace in this AMAZING home!

23. Live the Uptown urban lifestyle you crave!

24. Conference room, Pendant and track lighting, Garden bathtub, Pantry

25. Athletic center, Onsite storage facilities, Free gift wrapping station

26. This one has it all! Newer Construction with all the Bells & Whistles

27. Oh Yes We DID!!! OneBR/OneBA for $795/MO!!!

28. "Ritz Carlton" of Apartment Living!

29. We have the wonderful 2 bed/1.5 bath you've been waiting for!

30. Huge 2 Bed w/Massive Balcony & City Views

31. Gaga would go GAGA over this HUGE 2 bed/2 bath END UNIT!!!

32. Cats Welcome, Indoor bike racks, DVD Lending Library, Wooded views

33. ***** LARGE TOWNHOME, CLEAN AND UPDATED *****

CATCHY APARTMENT MARKETING SLOGANS

Whether it's winter, spring, summer, or fall, you need a list of clever, catchy apartment marketing slogans that are sure to get the attention of your prospects.

These slogans pack a great deal of power in just a few words. They're short, sophisticated, unique, and to the point.

1. You Can Afford To Dwell Well.

2. A Higher Quality of Living.

3. Apartments Tailored to Your Highest Standards.

4. At Last, This Is What You've Been Searching For.

5. Everything You Need. All Right Here.

6. Experience the [Apartment Name] Lifestyle.

7. Express Your Individuality at [Apartment Name].

8. Landmark Living on the Avenue.

9. Luxury All Around.

10. Luxury is Built-In. Not Tacked On.

11. Luxury, Location, and Convenience.

12. Modern Amenities. Urban Location. Sophisticated Style.

13. Proper Design. Smartly Priced. Ready for Move-In!

14. Remarkable Value. Unbeatable Location.

15. Right Around the Corner, Near Everywhere You Want to Be.

16. Service with a Lifestyle.

17. How to Live Better at [Apartment Name].

18. Iconic [Apartment Name] Living.

19. Commuter's Dream.

20. Don't Fuss with The Bus.

21. Life Just Got Better.

22. When Minutes Matter, Live Where You Work and Play

23. Where Convenience Meets Luxury.

24. Where Excellence and Convenience Meet.

25. Where Luxury and Convenience Converge.

26. Where Luxury City Living Reaches New Heights.

27. Where Luxury Meets Convenience.

28. Free Rent 'Til Next Year.

29. Warm Up with Our Hot Specials.

30. Always Fresh. Forever Original.

31. Beauty, Passion, Breathtaking Apartments.

32. Head-turning Style, Extraordinary Location.

33. Location, Community, Quality Living. It Starts Here!

34. Spectacular Views in Every Direction.

35. Stunning. Unique. And Very Upscale.

36. Supreme Residences for a Modern Lifestyle.

37. Spacious Modern Living.

38. The Epicenter of Luxury and Convenience.

39. The Lifestyle You Deserve.

40. The True Meaning of Luxury and Convenience.

41. Falling Leaves... Falling Prices! They're Both Happening at [Apartment Name].

42. Carve Out A Great Life at [Apartment Name].

43. City Outside. Tranquility Inside.

44. Discover Lakeside Apartment Living.

45. Unparalleled Views. Exceptional Style. Nonstop Luxury.

46. Urban Energy. Sky High Decadence.

47. Love Where You Live.

48. Live at the Center of Modern Conveniences & Entertainment.

49. Live Like You Want. That's Our Anthem.

50. Where the City Is Your Backyard.

51. New with a View.

52. Blending Relaxation & Sophistication to Create the Ideal Place.

53. A New Wave of Living.

54. Now Leasing! Instant Cool Factor.

55. Great Experiences Are Just Around The Corner.

56. It's Always Saturday at [Apartment Name].

57. Limitless Style, Unreal Service & Crazy Fun.

58. Live Outside The Lines.

59. Find Your Freedom, Without Leaving Home.

60. Sit Back, Relax. Your New View Awaits.

61. Modern Conveniences & Entertainment, All Within Your Reach.

62. Modern Living in the Heart of the City.

63. Sail Into Your New Home.

Want the Latest in Apartment Marketing?

There's a great deal of information covered in this book and many of these topics are discussed in depth in my weekly e-newsletter.

Join the community of over 4,000 multifamily professionals and get tips, tactics, and tutorials delivered to your inbox every Wednesday.

Visit **http://resident360.com/community** to check it out.

I'll see you there.

ACKNOWLEDGEMENTS

This second edition of *The Definitive Guide To Apartment Marketing* was really fun to create. I want to thank my mastermind group for keeping me accountable through the entire process—Henry, Christine, Kevin, Sandro, Vanessa, Travis, Aaron, Matt, and Jon.

Thanks to Michael Barrett, my co-founder at Resident360. Your constant, "When are you going to update this book," gave me the motivation I needed to get it done.

Thanks to my team at Resident360 for their input on several areas of this book, including the cover.

A special thanks to my wife, Natasha, and two sons, Jadson and Maxim—we did it again.

Finally, thank-you for reading the book and taking a real interest in apartment marketing. I wish you much success in all your marketing endeavors.

ABOUT THE AUTHOR

Josh Grillo is President of Resident360, a full service marketing agency specializing in Multifamily.

He brings his thirteen years' experience of building multimedia campaigns on television and the Internet to the multifamily industry. Josh has perfected a blend of Internet marketing combined with direct response triggers that give multifamily clients outstanding results.

He first started marketing on the Internet back in 2000, creating website products for ABC, NBC, CBS, and FOX local TV stations. By 2005, Josh created a new trend of marketing that leveraged local TV station brands to capture new advertisers. Combined with TV commercials, websites, vanity phone numbers, and Internet marketing this new trend generated over $50 million in revenue for clients in less than twenty-four months.

In 2008, when the recession hit, television advertisers pulled back on their spending, Josh took his business off air and worked directly with real estate and multifamily clients on Internet marketing and lead generation strategies.

Josh's motto is "results rule," and he works long and hard to make sure his clients are getting exceptional results. Many consider him an expert marketer and his strategies have been mentioned in the online edition of *The New York Times.* Josh is the absolute go-to guy for practical, proven marketing strategies for increasing occupancy.

Josh lives in San Diego with his amazing wife Natasha, his two sons, Jadson and Maxim, and their two Labrador retrievers Koa and Kona. He enjoys surfing, sailing, reading, and business.

His office is in San Diego, CA. Should you wish to contact him directly about marketing, consulting, speaking, or just comment about the book, please email him at josh@resident360.com or call his office at 855-360-9327. You can also visit his website at www.Resident360.com.

Made in the USA
Middletown, DE
19 August 2017